100
THINGS TO DO IN
PROVIDENCE
BEFORE YOU
DIE

Heather!
Tony! Abigail!
I hope you'll visit
me in PVD!

Rebecca Leo

100
THINGS TO DO IN
PROVIDENCE
BEFORE YOU
DIE

REBECCA KEISTER

Library of Congress Control Number: 2015957511

ISBN: 9781681060385

Design by Jill Halpin

Cover Photo Credit: GoProvidence/Nicholas Millard

Printed in the United States of America
16 17 18 19 20   5 4 3 2 1

Please note that websites, phone numbers, addresses, and company names are subject to change or cancellation. We did our best to relay the most accurate information available, but due to circumstances beyond our control, please do not hold us liable for misinformation. When exploring new destinations, please do your homework before you go.

DEDICATION

For my mother, my first and still strongest supporter
and the apple of my eye.

CONTENTS

PREFACE

A renaissance city. The "Creative Capital." A little city with a lot to offer. A place where most of us live off Hope (Street). Any one of these nicknames lovingly associated with Providence, Rhode Island, holds true. It's a city full of creative people, with a thriving arts economy and scene and a national reputation as a foodie's paradise. But it's so much more. I fell in love with Providence while on a press trip, sent here from a trade publication I worked for in Washington, D.C. Immersed in discovering the city's historical charm, culinary elegance, intellectual stimulation, stylish atmosphere, welcoming reception, and walkability, I easily saw how everyone, from undergraduates and young professionals to artists and families, loves living in this city bursting with unique, exciting, and adventurous opportunities. Readers familiar with Providence will undoubtedly recognize many of the places and activities in this book, but my hope is that they will revisit their favorite spots with fresh eyes and bring new friends to join the experience. Those considering a trip to Providence, which can easily fill a full week's vacation or a long weekend getaway, hopefully will find this guide as helpful to them as I found it enjoyable to write.

ACKNOWLEDGMENTS

This guide to Providence's charms and treasures would not have been possible without the support and cooperation of GoProvidence, the Providence-Warwick Convention & Visitors Bureau, especially Martha Sheridan and Kristen Adamo, two all-around brilliant travel professionals. Huge thanks go to all my online friends, especially members of the Providence Lady Project, who offered their favorite spots for consideration. Much appreciation goes to my family and friends for their unwavering support and faith in me and my writing. Finally, my thanks go to everyone in Providence and everywhere who choose to live off hope.

Welcome to
Historic
Federal Hill

FOOD AND DRINK

INDULGE IN A CULINARY TOUR
OF FEDERAL HILL

A pineapple-adorned archway leads visitors into the city's Italian center, where restaurants, bakeries, and shops offer a taste of old-world charms and treats. In fact, so many delectable dining and shopping options are available that choosing just one spot can be overwhelming. Chef Cindy Salvo's "Savoring Federal Hill" culinary tour not only allows a sampling of some of the neighborhood's famed local establishments but also meet-and-greets with the chefs and shop owners. During the three-hour walking and eating tour, Chef Salvo also shares her Italian cooking tips and how to use products you can pick up in Federal Hill markets. You'll also visit the Federal Hill wine shop that Salvo says brought Italian wines and spirits to New England. Bonus: Tours are limited to fourteen people, ensuring an immersive experience.

Savoring Rhode Island
Tours meet at Federal Hill's DePasquale Plaza on Atwells Avenue or inside nearby Café Dolce Vita, dependent on season. Tours are $50 per person.
401-934-2149
savoringrhodeisland.com

TIP

Salvo advises bringing along a cooler
for meats, cheeses, and other treats you'll
want to purchase during the tour.

FEAST ON FISH
AT THE RHODE ISLAND SEAFOOD FESTIVAL

It's hard to describe the Rhode Island Seafood Festival accurately other than to say that if fish is your preferred dish, get yourself there immediately. Well, you'll have to wait until summer, as this event for seafood lovers is held annually in mid-September at India Point Park. Vendors include some of the Ocean State's best and most popular seafood restaurants, including Matunuck Oyster Bar and the Shuckin Truck seafood truck whose sea scallop roll is a regular crowd favorite. Other than the most seafood offered in one place in Rhode Island, the festival includes beer and wine as well as live music all day, each day of the two-day festival. The festival is held rain or shine, but with such a yummy lineup, you likely won't mind a few sprinkles.

Rhode Island Seafood Festival
263 India St., 845-222-7469
riseafoodfest.com

GRAB A FOOD TRUCK LUNCH
AT KENNEDY PLAZA

Even Providence's busiest movers and shakers need a lunch break, and many of them regularly head to Kennedy Plaza, downtown's epicenter that provides breathtaking views of the city skyline day and night, for the Food Truck Market. A Kennedy Plaza staple since 2010, the Food Truck Market serves lunch during the workweek (Monday through Friday) with a rotating lineup of delectable cuisine options, with the occasional dinnertime offering. Partakers can find such lunches as gourmet pretzel sandwiches from Noble Knots, from-scratch burgers from Rocket Fine Street Food, authentic Mexican dishes from Poco Loco Tacos, and crepes you'd swear were straight from Paris from O'Crepe, among many others. Grab a couple of coworkers, head out on a sunny day, and enjoy a well-deserved and fresh daytime break.

Food Truck Market at Kennedy Plaza
Kennedy Plaza (between Providence City Hall, 25 Dorrance St., and the Providence Federal Building, 380 Westminster St.), 401-521-8800
provparksconservancy.org/visit/food-trucks

DISCOVER THE BEERS THE LOCALS CRAVE
AT THE RHODE ISLAND BREW FEST

This annual festival, traditionally held during the winter at the nearby Pawtucket Armory, allows beer connoisseurs to sample craft brews from over fifty Rhode Island breweries. Guests purchase tickets for one of two three-hour sampling sessions at the festival. With over 170 brews to chose from, from traditional IPAS to dark stouts, there's something everyone is sure to love and discover from Ocean State breweries. Guests also take home a souvenir pint glass or beer goblet. The festival features vendors and a food court, with many locally produced treats as well as live music. Run by Gray Matter Marketing, the festival supports its vendors by eliminating booth rental fees and paying breweries to showcase their beers. Each year a portion of the proceeds goes to support the Rhode Island Brewers Guild.

Rhode Island Brew Fest
Pawtucket Armory
172 Exchange St., Pawtucket
ribrewfest.com

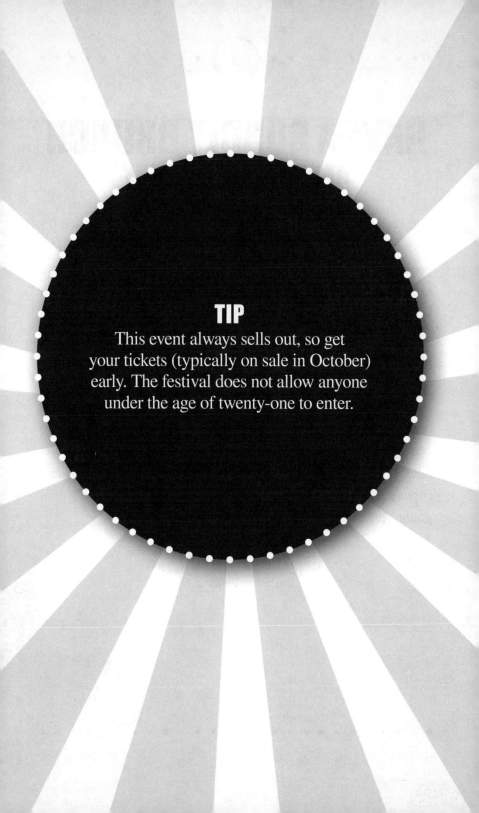

TIP

This event always sells out, so get your tickets (typically on sale in October) early. The festival does not allow anyone under the age of twenty-one to enter.

HAVE A BUBBLY BRUNCH
AT THE DUCK & BUNNY

They call it a snuggery—a "cozy and comfortable place"—and it's easy to see why. Step into the Duck & Bunny and you feel like you're in someone's really yummy-smelling home. In fact, the restaurant was someone's home and has been reimagined as a "sanctuary away from the noise" with some of the house's original charm in place, including fireplaces that keep you cozy during winter months. Serving up brunch daily, the snuggery features crepes and specialties that incorporate local favorites, including its award-winning sweetbread pudding benny (Portuguese sweet bread pudding topped with traditional eggs Benedict). Those who can't get enough of the restaurant's eclectic atmosphere and menu flock here after brunch for its beer-and-wine-based cocktails and cupcakes, which are baked on-site daily and feature vegan and gluten-free options.

The Duck & Bunny
312 Wickenden St., 401-270-3300
theduckandbunny.com

FIND YOUR INNER CHEF
AT A JOHNSON & WALES UNIVERSITY CHEF'S CHOICE CLASS

Providence is lucky to be home to one of the nation's leading collegiate culinary programs at Johnson & Wales University and even luckier that the university offers chef's choice classes taught by the school's professional chef instructors and geared toward cooks of all levels. Budding chefs get instructor demonstrations and hands-on experience—plus the bonus of tasting their hard work—in a variety of genres during three-hour classes. Class takers can choose between knife skills, global cuisines, holiday baking, Pasta 101, food and wine pairing, and much more. Classes range from $85 to around $150 per person. The university also offers a certified wine specialist class that starts at $250. Classes are limited to those ages sixteen and up. Wine-and-beer-specific classes are limited to those ages twenty-one and older. The school also offers classes for children and teens.

Johnson & Wales University
8 Abbott Park Place, 401-598-2336
jwu.edu

SIP A CUP OF COFFEE MILK
AT DAVE'S COFFEE

When ordering this Rhode Island–born beverage, make sure you pronounce it "kaw-fee" milk or risk outing yourself as a tourist or Ocean State transplant, though you'll be welcome just the same as the locals are at Dave's Coffee on South Main Street, the gourmet coffee bar that Dave's Coffee Roasting Co. had the good sense to establish as an East Side hangout in recent years. Rhode Island's official state beverage, kaw-fee milk is a coffee-syrup-sweetened beverage, and Dave's Coffee makes the best coffee syrup around. A bonus is that everything in the syrup minus Brazilian coffee beans is made right in Rhode Island. A second bonus is that everything Dave's Coffee serves—from a full range of coffees to giant pastries—is just as tasty as its signature product.

Dave's Coffee
341 South Main St., 401-322-0006
davescoffeestore.com

TIP

Don't forget to snap up a bottle of coffee syrup to take home so that you can keep enjoying this treat.

SUCCUMB TO DEATH BY CHOCOLATE
AT GREGG'S RESTAURANT

If it's good enough for the president of the United States, surely it's worth a stop during your Providence trip. President Barack Obama made the restaurant's already famous chocolate layer cake a VIP treat when he stopped in to grab a slice during a visit to a local college in 2014. Gregg's calls the dessert a chocoholic's dream come true. With four layers of moist cake alternated with dark chocolate fudge icing and chocolate curls on top, one can hardly argue their point. The cake also has been voted best in the state by *Rhode Island Monthly* readers twelve years in a row and is available during your meal or as a take-home dessert. And if this treat isn't enough to tempt you, Gregg's also offers a supersized version called Death by Chocolate Cake.

Gregg's Restaurant & Pub
1303 N Main St., 401-831-5700
greggsusa.com

GET A LATE-NIGHT SNACK FIX
AT HAVEN BROTHERS DINER

You haven't truly experienced Providence's nightlife until you visit the Haven Brothers Diner, a food truck offering diner menu classics to college students and other after-midnight patrons. The menu is full of greasy goodness, including hamburgers, hot dogs, chili, and more. Favorites include the Murder Burger, a double-deckerbeef patty with bacon, mayo, mushrooms, and grilled onions, and the Haven Dog, a wiener topped with bacon, mustard, relish, onions, ketchup, chili, and cheese. The truck is parked downtown next to Providence City Hall from 4:30 p.m. to 5 a.m. each day, making its almost historic dishes available even to early birds. The Haven Brothers Diner was established as a horse-drawn lunch wagon in 1888, making it one of the country's oldest operating food trucks.

Haven Brothers Diner
Next to Providence City Hall, 25 Dorrance St.
facebook.com/pages/Haven-Brothers/133645720026940

BITE INTO A WIENER
AT OLNEYVILLE NEW YORK SYSTEM

Whether you prefer it "all the way" (with the works) or simply with the scrumptious sauce available only at Olneyville New York System, a hot wiener is a Rhode Island favorite you can't leave the city without trying. The restaurant has been around since the 1930s when Nicolas Stevens and his father, Anthony, moved their operation from Brooklyn, New York, where they'd been running a candy shop since emigrating from Greece a decade earlier. Brooklyn's loss certainly was Providence's gain. Olneyville New York System has been at its Plainfield Street locale since 1953 and has been serving the best wieners in town since that time. You'll probably also want to take home some of the packaged hot wiener sauce—the restaurant's signature blend of six spices that you add to its recommended 80 percent (or less) ground beef—so you can whip up a taste of Rhode Island after your visit.

Olneyville New York System
18 Plainfield St., 401-621-9500
olneyvillenewyorksystem.com

TIP

The restaurant stays open until 2 a.m. Sunday through Thursday and 3 a.m. on Friday and Saturday for late-night revelers.

SIP A SUMMER COCKTAIL
AT THE HOT CLUB

The Hot Club is this restaurant/bar's actual name, and it really is the city's "it" place to relax after a long summer's day or during a long summer's day, as it's really easy to pass the time sipping a cocktail or beer at this waterfront spot. A relatively small indoor bar is available, but you're going to want to hang out on the adjoining dock that stands over the Providence River to really enjoy the summery atmosphere. Sitting, or more likely standing due to the bar's outstanding popularity, on the deck and looking out at the city skyline is one of the best views available in Providence. It's easy to see why the bar has been used as a Hollywood filming location several times, including for the Showtime series *Brotherhood*.

The Hot Club
575 South Water St., 401-861-9007
hotclubprov.com

TOMATO, TOMATO
AT CHEZ PASCAL

It's a tomato fiesta during the annual Tomato Dinner at Chez Pascal, a charming and cozy French restaurant on the city's East Side. For thirteen years and counting, Chez Pascal has had this dinner every August, with five courses each featuring the tomato as a main incorporation, and has consistently delivered unique dishes each year. The dinner is reasonably priced (in 2014, it was $73 per person without gratuity), and its popularity (it sells out quickly) is likely due to the restaurant's reputation as the place to enjoy a Parisian-inspired menu in Providence. Run by a pair who met while working at a Boston bistro, the restaurant features an ever-changing menu to focus on local produce, including the tomato.

Chez Pascal
960 Hope St., 401-421-4442
chez-pascal.com

TIP
Chez Pascal is not able to accommodate dietary restrictions at this event.

STAR CHEF'S SERIES
AT GRACIE'S

One of many fine-dining Providence restaurants to work its menu around seasonal harvests, Gracie's, a four-diamond restaurant downtown, takes it up a notch by using many ingredients from its own rooftop garden. But the restaurant doesn't stop there. For seven years, Gracie's has invited star chefs from across the country to host a tasting menu in cooperation with its executive chef and pastry chef. Star chef guests have included the culinary director of Robert Sinskey Vineyards in Napa, California, and the executive chef and owner of LOLA in Great Neck, New York, to name just two. A Star Chef's Series dinner is a decadent treat. Tickets are around $150 per person, but the experience, like every Gracie's meal, is one you'll never forget.

Gracie's
194 Washington St., 401-272-7811
graciesprov.com

MEET PROVIDENCE'S MIXOLOGISTS
AT THE EDDY

In recent years, Providence has embraced the mixologist/speakeasy craze, and bars featuring craft cocktails and a 1920s vibe have popped up around the city. The Eddy has emerged as the cream of this crop. Located downtown and open only at night (or after 4 p.m.) and serving snacks until 11:30 p.m., the Eddy regularly draws a packed crowd to its smallish quarters that feature a U-shaped bar and dapperly dressed mixologists who rotate a featured drinks menu and who are happy to craft you a custom concoction based on your cocktail preferences. The limited menu often rotates as well, offering an eclectic mix of nibbles that range from tater tots to deviled eggs and oysters.

The Eddy
95 Eddy St., 401-831-3339
eddybar.com

THE BEST BURGERS AROUND
AT HARRY'S BAR & BURGER

Providence has been dubbed a best burgers city by *Travel + Leisure* magazine, reaching number one on its 2012 list. You can choose from many excellent burger joints, but favorites include Harry's Bar & Burger, which exclusively uses certified Hereford beef and makes its burgers by hand each day— nothing frozen here—with its special sauce and your pick of topping combinations. If you happen to go with someone who doesn't love burgers, the menu offers much more, including a scrumptious chili. Leave room for the Irish car bomb brownie bites, a classic dessert with a boozy twist.

Harry's Bar & Burger—two locations
121 N Main St., 401-228-7437
301 Atwells Ave., 401-228-3336
harrysbarburger.com

EXPERIENCE BOB & TIMMY'S
"LEGENDARY" GRILLED PIZZA

In a foodie city where you almost can't go wrong, it's hard to become known as the go-to eatery for a local specialty, but one trip to Bob & Timmy's and one bite of their grilled pizza will make you a believer in the next to impossible. A Federal Hill favorite, Bob & Timmy's serves the locally famous grilled pizza—a thin crust grilled on an open wood fire—in a variety of specialty combinations, including the chicken alfredo and trio of wild mushrooms pizza. Traditional cheese toppings more your thing? Not to worry, as they have this too, and it's delicious. The restaurant has two additional locations in Smithfield, Rhode Island, and nearby North Attleboro, Massachusetts.

Bob & Timmy's Grilled Pizza
32 Spruce St., 401-453-2221
bobandtimmys.com

FEEL YOUNG AGAIN
AT WICKENDEN PUB

Wickenden Street is a main college hangout drag for bar hopping, and lots of young residents flock to Wickenden Pub, a neighborhood watering hole where if you visit more than once most people are likely to know your name. Locals know this is always a lively place to watch Sunday football or to unwind on a Friday evening. Craft beer lovers adore the bar's Beer Club, featuring ninety-nine different brews to try and giving victors a plaque on its wall, and cocktail lovers are treated to well-balanced favorites. There's tons of weekly specials too, so take advantage of such things as Dollar Off Mondays (beer) and Super Raffle Thursday. So pull up a barstool and join the crowd that believes beer makes everything better. Oh, only if you're twenty-one or older, though, of course.

Wickenden Pub
320 Wickenden St., 401-861-2555
facebook.com/wickendenpub

TRY A DIFFERENT DISH
EVERY NIGHT DURING RESTAURANT WEEK

Twice per year—in January and July—many Providence restaurants participate in restaurant week and offer two-course lunches and three-course dinners at bargain prices. Created to draw business during slower spending months, the chance to enjoy world-class cuisine and try innovative dishes has diners flocking to restaurants all over the city each night during restaurant week. From favorites, such as the Old Canteen on Atwells Avenue, to hot new downtown spots, such as Circle on Weybosset Street, you can't go wrong in choosing any one of the participating eateries. Lunches offer a main course and dessert, and dinner adds an appetizer to that menu with all restaurants offering diners plenty of delectable choices. GoProvidence, the city's convention and visitors bureau, starts advertising participating restaurants weeks in advance, and reservations are recommended.

Providence Restaurant Week
Various locations
goprovidence.com/restaurantweek

JOIN THE ZEPPOLE CRAZE
AT LASALLE BAKERY

Providence residents celebrate St. Joseph's Day (the feast day for Saint Joseph, husband of the Virgin Mary) but feast on zeppole, an Italian pastry so decadent and so delicious you'll want to eat them year-round, and the best of the bunch are at LaSalle Bakery. Here, you can get a zeppola (singular for zeppole) traditionally made of a deep-fried ball of dough, filled with a variety of gooey goodness, including pastry cream or custard, and topped with powdered sugar and a cherry. LaSalle Bakery often has specialty takes on the treat, including a Guinness-themed zeppola. The bakery prides itself on an "old-school, old-world, no-shortcut" baking manifesto that customers appreciate in its out-of-this world baked goods.

LaSalle Bakery—two locations
993 Smith St., 401-831-9563
685 Admiral St., 401-228-0881
lasallebakery.net

TIP

Zeppole Day draws a crowd. Try to go as early as possible, but be prepared to wait in line no matter the hour.

VISIT SOUTHERN ITALY
AT ZOOMA TRATTORIA

Zooma Trattoria on Federal Hill distinguishes itself as the only Italian restaurant in Providence offering dishes crafted in the Mediterranean tradition of southern Italy, from pizza Napoletana to its Gnocchi a la nonna. Everything on the menu, which can change subject to availability of local ingredients, is made to order. The restaurant's pasta is made fresh on the premises daily. Must-tries include Nonna's gnocchi and the tortellini viso roso (goat cheese–filled red wine tortellini). The wine list here is tops among Federal Hill establishments. With an atmosphere of welcoming sophistication, it's a popular spot for after-work drinks and romantic dinners. The restaurant hosts monthly wine dinners, chef's tastings, and other special events as well.

Zooma Trattoria
245 Atwells Ave., 401-383-2002
trattoriazoomari.com

TIP
Zooma is a best bet for a quick but elegant lunch offering a three-course lunch Monday through Friday prepared to get you back to work on time.

VINO, PLEASE

Yes, it is possible to make good wine in Rhode Island, and a full slate of wineries are available to prove it. They are far apart, so it's not likely you could visit all of them within a day unless you had arranged transportation, which would be a great way to taste our grapes in style. Whether you like white or red, bold or delicate, sparkling or dessert wine, you'll likely find something you love at one of these vineyards.

Carolyn's Sakonnet Vineyard
162 W Main Rd., Little Compton, 401-635-8486
sakonnetwine.com

Greenvale Vineyards
582 Wapping Rd., Portsmouth, 401-847-3777
greenvale.com

Newport Vineyards
909 E Main Rd., Middletown, 401-848-5161
newportvineyards.com

Nickle Creek Vineyard
12 King Rd., Foster, 401-369-3694
nicklecreekvineyard.com

Leyden Farm Vineyard and Winery
160 Plain Meeting House Rd., West Greenwich, 401-392-1133
leydenfarm.com

Langworthy Farm
308 Shore Rd., Westerly, 401-322-7791
langworthyfarm.com

Purple Cat Vineyard and Winery
11 Money Hill Rd., Chepachet, 401-566-9463
purplecatwinery.com

Verde Vineyards
50 Hopkins Ave., Johnston, 401-934-2317
verdevineyardsri.com

TASTE THE AWESOME AWFUL AWFUL
AT NEWPORT CREAMERY

Despite its iconic moniker, Newport Creamery's Awful Awful is one tasty treat unlike any other kind of frozen ice cream drink that any Providence visitor has got to try. You'll recognize the flavored syrup and milk, but the secret is the frozen ice milk mix that Newport Creamery isn't sharing. You can get yours flavored strawberry, vanilla, chocolate mint, or coffee or go for the Outrageous Awful Awful with Oreo, Strawberry Banana Chip, Cappuccino Crunch & Choc O'Nutter. Both the original and outrageous versions are available in junior size, but you'll definitely want all you can get after the first frozen drop.

Newport Creamery
Various locations
newportcreamery.com

SAMPLE THE STATE'S BEST
AT THE EAT DRINK
RHODE ISLAND FESTIVAL

Local blogger David Dadekian has been keeping Providence residents up to date on the city's latest culinary trends, news, and events on eatdrinkri.com since 2010 and complements his writing with an annual festival that showcases the state's best foods, beverages, chef's and more. The festival's main event is a grand tasting that typically samples about forty local vendors and has in the past included presentations by Rhode Island's best chefs. The festival also hosts a special multicourse dinner cooked by several different Rhode Island chefs, a food truck stop at a central city location, and a grand brunch that features dishes, cocktails, and desserts from some of the state's most popular brunch spots. The festival is usually held the first weekend in May.

Eat Drink Rhode Island Festival
eatdrinkri.com

sandra feinstein-

GAM

theatre

MUSIC AND ENTERTAINMENT

TAKE IN A BROADWAY SHOW
AT THE PROVIDENCE PERFORMING ARTS CENTER

The Providence Performing Arts Center, the unofficial heart of the city's arts and entertainment district, is a sight to behold inside and out. Walking up to the thirty-one-hundred-seat theater, you'd swear you were in New York, especially when its old-fashioned marquee lights up the night. Inside, theatergoers are treated to 1920s opulence. The theater has been meticulously remodeled and restored to reflect its original elegance. Built in 1928, the theater is on the National Register of Historic Places and previously housed a movie palace. Today, it's a favorite for Broadway show tours, pre-Broadway runs, and national tour openings. An especially stylish time to visit is during the winter holiday season, when the theater is fully decked in Christmas decor.

Providence Performing Arts Center
220 Weybosset St., 401-421-2787
ppacri.org

EXPERIENCE INTIMATE THEATER
AT TRINITY REPERTORY COMPANY AND THE GAMM

Providence's Trinity Repertory Company and Pawtucket's Sandra Feinstein-Gamm Theatre both provide unparalleled acting troupes with seasons featuring a wide range of productions, from screwball comedies to Tennessee Williams classics and Shakespeare. Trinity Rep, as it's called, is a member of the League of Resident Theatres and is highly regarded nationwide as one of the best regional theaters around. The Gamm, as it's called, originally operated in Providence's Jewelry District before finding new life at Pawtucket's Armory Center inside an old police garage. Each theater gives patrons an up-close-to-the-stage experience rarely found in such highly esteemed venues.

Trinity Repertory Company
201 Washington St., 401-351-4242
trinityrep.com

Sandra Feinstein-Gamm Theatre
172 Exchange St., Pawtucket, 401-723-4266
gammtheatre.org

GET YOUR FASHIONISTA FIX
AT STYLEWEEK NORTHEAST

You don't need to travel to Paris, Milan, or even New York to see the next season's fashions sashay down the runway. StyleWeek Northeast is a biannual event of five to seven days' worth of fashion-forward celebrations of design, innovation, and beauty. One of the country's few regional fashion weeks, the event was created in 2009 to showcase emerging designers, and it's done just that, in the process gaining a loyal following of fashionistas who gather for runway shows, an accessories showcase, cocktail hours, and an after-party. It's been highly successful in connecting designers with industry insiders and press and is also highly covered in local publications, so you may just get your picture in the paper. Runway shows are ticketed and require check-ins.

StyleWeek Northeast
65 Weybosset St., Unit 122, 781-816-7963
styleweeknortheast.com

FLICKERS: RHODE ISLAND
INTERNATIONAL FILM FESTIVAL

Movie buffs, this one's for you. The FLICKERS: Rhode Island International Film Festival—taking place largely in Providence but throughout the state—has been one of few regional festivals to feature works of "any type, on any subject matter, and in any genre." Attendees have a huge range of films (in the several hundreds) to choose from, including documentaries, animation, and drama. It's a full-fledged juried competition of independent films from around the world. It's been a qualifying event for the Academy of Motion Pictures awards in the short film and documentary short categories, and features several events in addition to screenings, including a script-writing contest, a master class on filmmaking, and filmmaking forums. The festival traditionally takes place in August.

FLICKERS: Rhode Island International Film Festival
83 Park St., #5, 401-861-4445
film-festival.org

TAKE IN A MOVIE
AT CABLE CAR CINEMA

This East Side theater is where Providence moviegoers choose to view independent films when they really want to relax while taking in a movie. That's because in place of standard movie seats, Cable Car Cinema has comfy couches built for one, two, or three, but a few extra-nice standard-type seats are also available. It's got that arthouse feel, with distinctive wall murals and movie posters galore inside its charmingly small space. The cinema cafe serves reasonably priced sandwiches, salads, and pastries as well as wine and beer.

Cable Car Cinema and Cafe
204 South Main St., 401-272-3970
cablecarcinema.com

BALLET, MUSIC, AND MORE
AT VETERANS MEMORIAL AUDITORIUM

The Veterans Memorial Auditorium, simply called "the Vets" by locals, straddles the Hill and downtown areas on Providence's Avenue of the Arts. A majestic exterior complements the venue's interior grandeur, which includes a ceiling adorned with shields from the thirty-nine original Rhode Island communities. Visitors marvel at the auditorium's acoustics and grand stage. The Vets is home to the Rhode Island Philharmonic and Festival Ballet Providence (which performs *The Nutcracker* annually) and is a venue for the FLICKERS: Rhode Island International Film Festival. Many more shows are staged here, including musical acts of all genres, ranging from classical to contemporary and comedy shows. The theater, originally intended to be a Masonic building operated by the Freemasons, is on the National Register of Historic Places.

Veterans Memorial Auditorium
1 Avenue of the Arts, 401-421-2787
vmari.com

JOIN THE LOCAL ARTS COMMUNITY
AT AS220

Located downtown, AS220 is like an artist's paradise that's open for the public to enjoy. Local artists (of all mediums) find opportunities here to live, work, exhibit, and perform while, in turn, the public finds opportunities to enjoy the work of those artists. AS220 is an artist-run organization focused on providing a space for artists to do all this when they are limited by lack of affordable opportunities elsewhere. They have a gallery, performance stage, dance studio, a black-box theater, print shop, and darkroom among other spaces. AS220 also has a great little restaurant/bar, which features one of the city's best vegetarian/vegan menus.

AS220
115 Empire St., 401-831-9327
as220.org

LISTEN AND LAUGH
AT THE DUELING PIANOS

Celebrating a birthday? Bachelor/bachelorette party? In need of a laugh-filled night out? Head on over to Point Street Dueling Pianos. Shows feature two pianist/singers who play audience requests. Audience clapping and singing is more than encouraged. You can—and should—request a person to be brought on stage where it's all in good fun but helped by a good spirit. Audiences love the good-humored pianists. The pianists love a good-humored audience. It's a win-win here when everybody comes to play. Reservations are a good idea, though walk-ins are welcome, and the cover is inexpensive. If you've got a really large party (more than thirty), you can arrange for catering. Point Street Dueling Pianos is open Wednesday through Saturday.

Point Street Dueling Pianos
3 Davol Square, 401-270-7828
pointstreetpianos.com

DISCOVER LOCAL BANDS
AT THE MET, THE PARLOUR, THE SPOT UNDERGROUND, DUSK, AND FÊTE

Providence has a kickin' indie music scene with stellar bands that play a range of music, from folk to heavy metal, though there's a leaning toward alternative rock. These venues regularly host multiact shows put on by some of Providence's best up-and-coming talent.

The Met
1005 Main St., Pawtucket, 401-729-1005
themetri.com

The Parlour
1119 N Main St., 401-383-5858
theparlourri.com

The Spot Underground
180 Pine St., 401-383-7133
thespotunderground.com

Dusk
301 Harris Ave., 401-714-0444
duskprovidence.com

Fête Music Hall
103 Dike St., 401-383-1112
fetemusic.com

GO BACK IN TIME
AT BREAKTIME BOWL & BAR

Step back into the 1920s at this speakeasy-designed bowling alley and bar in Pawtucket's Hope Artiste Village. Everything inside is vintage designed, from the six bowling lanes with individual old-school (hand-run) setters to the fully stocked bar. The bowling alley has a rustic feel but a welcoming, cozy vibe and offers an upscale pub-style menu with something sure to satisfy the taste buds of everyone in your party. The alley is a restoration of a bowling alley used by labor movement workers at the Hope Webbing Mill and takes its name from the fact that those workers used the alley as a community gathering spot during their break times from work. True to its '20s theme, you'll be bowling duckpin here, and you'll be having a roaring good time doing it.

Breaktime Bowl & Bar
999 Main St., #1330, Pawtucket, 844-467-3383
breaktimebowlandbar.com

HAVE A SPOOKY GOOD TIME
ON THE PROVIDENCE GHOST TOUR

Plenty of chills and thrills—of the historical nature—await you on the Providence Ghost Tour. The tour was designed from meticulous research and is about an hour-and-a-half guided walk of East Side buildings and houses thought to be haunted based on records of unusual (or non-natural) deaths that happened in those locations. There's nothing gimmicky going on here, but because the narration discusses murder among other unnatural deaths, the tour is not appropriate for children. You'll get a strong dose of Providence history that's especially interesting to those who like a little dose of paranormal activity. The tours are offered June through November.

Providence Ghost Tour
60 Congdon St., 401-484-8687
providenceghosttour.com

CHEER ON THE GIRLS
AT THE PROVIDENCE ROLLER DERBY

New England's first all-female roller derby league is a five-team league (three home teams and two travel teams) that started in 2004. The nonprofit organization strives to positively impact the lives of skaters and the skater community and bring awareness to the sport. Women's flat-track roller derby features two teams of five members skating in the same direction along a track with one player from each team designated as the jammer, who tries to score points while warding off the other team's efforts to stall her progress. It can get rowdy, and roaring cheers from the audience are part of the fun. Providence Roller Derby teams play in Providence, Narragansett, and Warwick during a season that typically goes from March through October.

Providence Roller Derby
P.O. Box 2516
providencerollerderby.com

TEST YOUR USELESS INFO IQ
AT TRIVIA NIGHT AT CHELOS

Chelos is one of those unofficial state landmarks, with locations throughout the state that draw nightly crowds to its bar and dining room. You could certainly play pub trivia—the popular bar game that encourages expert knowledge in random facts in all imaginable subjects—at many places in Providence, but doing so at Chelos ensures a good meal and a good chance to make friends with locals. Chelos's Providence location hosts trivia on Tuesday nights.

Chelos Hometown Bar & Grille
505 Silver Spring St., 401-861-6644
chelos.com

MAKE YOUR OWN
MOVIE TOUR

Did you know Providence, R.I. has been used as a filming location for several blockbuster and indie movies as well as many high-profile TV shows? Such big-name stars as Joaquin Phoenix, Katherine Heigl, and Mark Ruffalo have all walked this city's streets filming such titles as *An Irrational Man*, *27 Dresses*, and *Infinitely Polar Bear*. Though the state doesn't—yet anyway—have a vendor offering a guided tour of these locations, it's easy enough to design your own and stand where the stars stood while they were in town.

Suggested Stops and Their Star-Studded Associations

An Irrational Man: West Side Diner, 1380 Westminster St., 401-490-0644
westsidedinerri.com

27 Dresses: Mills Tavern,101 N Main St., 401 272-3331
millstavernrestaurant.com

Showtime's *Brotherhood*: McCormick & Schmick's Seafood & Steaks,
11 Dorrance St., 401-351-4500
mccormickandschmicks.com

Infinitely Polar Bear: Wayland Manor, 500 Angell St., 401 751 7700

Dan in Real Life: Seven Stars Bakery, 820 Hope St., 401-521-2200
sevenstarsbakery.com

There's Something About Mary: The Hot Club, 575 South Water St.,
401-861-9007
hotclubprov.com

GET CULTURED
AT THE RHODE ISLAND
PHILHARMONIC ORCHESTRA

For more than seventy years, starting in 1944, the Rhode Island Philharmonic Orchestra has delighted audiences with its world-class symphony orchestra that plays classical and pops concerts. Performing at the Vets, the orchestra's season features an eight-concert classical series, the Amica Rush Hour Series (held on early Friday evenings) that presents shorter classical concerts, and four open rehearsals where audiences can witness the magic that happens between the orchestra, conductor, and guest artists. The orchestra also plays education and in-school concerts. The orchestra's music school is the state's sole such school and offers programs to people of all ages, incomes, and playing abilities and has a focus on providing opportunities to engage students in orchestra.

Rhode Island Philharmonic Orchestra & Music School
667 Waterman Ave., East Providence, 401-248-7070
riphil.org

CATCH A FLICK WITH YOUR NEIGHBORS
AT MOVIES ON THE BLOCK

Every summer from June through September Grant Block in downtown turns into a bona fide block party with Movies on the Block. Run by InDowncity (a merchant's association) and Cornish Associates (a real estate group), Movies on the Block is a free community event. The usual summer lineup includes something for everyone, from cartoons to classics and thrillers, and it's a great nighttime treat for most kids in your life. With no provided seating, it's best to get to the party early. Grab takeout from one of the neighboring restaurants, and mark your territory with a blanket or beach chair. Then enjoy your dinner al fresco while waiting for the show to start.

Movies on the Block
260 Westminster St.
moviesontheblock.com

ROCK OUT
AT THE COLUMBUS THEATRE

History and music await you at the Columbus Theatre, a West End neighborhood concert hall that originally hosted vaudeville acts and played silent films in the late 1920s. The hall also was once the city's go-to movie house, operated by RKO Albee Theatre in the post–World War II days and a beloved community arts venue before reopening in 2012 as a concert hall. Now run by the Columbus Cooperative, the Columbus Theatre focuses on staging a "range of unique live events in an unequaled space." Two theaters (seating two hundred and eight hundred people) offer an event schedule featuring local artists and touring bands. Community events, such as lager release parties, are also held here. Be aware that the theater's bar is cash only and there's no parking lot, though on-street parking is fairly easily found.

Columbus Theatre
270 Broadway St., 401-621-9660
columbustheatre.com

HAVE A JAZZY NIGHT
AT ASPIRE

During summer months, the courtyard at Aspire Seasonal Kitchen in the city's downtown area is transformed into a swinging jazz club where the famous Joe Potenza Quartet, which features a rotating list of guests stars (the world-renowned saxophonist Greg Abate has been known to appear), play from 7:30 to 11 each Friday night. It's the perfect spot to mingle with a martini, relax with a glass from the restaurant's superb wine list, or simply sit back and tap your feet to the tunes. There's jazz at Aspire every Friday night, but summer in the courtyard is the best time. There's no cover charge for the show, and the kitchen serves up some of the city's best small plates.

Aspire Seasonal Kitchen
311 Westminster St., 401-521-3333
aspirerestaurant.com

DRIVE ON IN
TO THE RUSTIC TRI VUE DRIVE-IN

Are you someone whose smile gets wider when the old-fashioned concession stand commercials play at the movies—you know, the ones with the dancing popcorn and soda? If so, a night at the movies under the stars at the Rustic Tri Vue Drive-In on Eddie Dowling Highway in North Smithfield will tickle your fancy more than any multiplex. Designed in authentic 1950s style (starting with the roadside sign), the drive-in has three screens that play two films each on show nights starting at dusk. A full concession stand features clam cakes, hot dogs, chicken tenders, and the like as well as a self-serve ice cream shop and a great sound system streamed through car stereos. The drive-in is open April through September, with some special movie nights around Halloween.

Rustic Tri Vue Drive-In
1195 Eddie Dowling Highway, North Smithfield, 401-769-7601
yourneighborhoodtheatre.com

CATCH A CONCERT
AT WATERPLACE PARK

Summer in the city is filled with opportunities to experience all Providence arts has to offer, including the free concert series held at Waterplace Park, which, with Riverwalk, is an "urban panorama" that features walkways with cobblestones and pedestrian bridges. You'll feel as though you're walking on water in the middle of the city. The city of Providence, the Department of Art, Culture + Tourism, and 95.5 WBRU team up each summer to stage the Friday night series that features local talent and alternative rock groups. As it's free, the shows are totally open and all ages are welcome. If you want a good seat, be sure to get there early.

Waterplace Park
401-272-9550
wbru.com

Photo Credit: GoProvidence/Nicholas Millard

SPORTS AND RECREATION

CHEER ON THE PROVIDENCE BRUINS
AT THE DUNKIN' DONUTS CENTER

The American Hockey League affiliate of the Boston Bruins, the Providence Bruins play their home games at the Dunkin' Donuts Center, an indoor arena that can host 11,075 fans for ice hockey games. Providence has had the fortune to host minor league hockey since 1992, after infamous then-mayor Buddy Cianci made it happen by moving the Maine Mariners franchise here, though the city also was home to the Providence Reds from 1972 to 1977. The Bruins won their first (and so far only) AHL Calder Cup in 1999, but win or lose, the game is a guaranteed good time.

Dunkin' Donuts Center
One LaSalle Square, 401-331-6700
providencebruins.com

ICE-SKATE UNDER THE STARS
AT THE ALEX AND ANI CITY CENTER

Picture an ideal New England winter's night. The air is crisp but not too cool, you're swirling and gliding across ice, and holding hands with someone special. Then, it begins to snow. While perfect wintery weather isn't a guarantee, there's always magic in the air while ice-skating around the rink at the Alex and Ani City Center, which, at fourteen thousand square feet, is twice the size of the rink at Rockefeller Center. So, lace up, warm up, and make some memories. Ice-skating begins in late November and runs through mid-March.

Alex and Ani City Center
2 Kennedy Plaza, 401-331-5544
alexandanicitycenter.com

PAMPER YOURSELF
AT THE SPA AT THE
PROVIDENCE BILTMORE

Taking in all of Providence might leave you a bit weary and in need of some relaxation in the form of a facial, massage, or pedicure. Step on into the Spa at the Providence Biltmore, where luxury awaits. The spa is located inside the equally elegant Providence Biltmore, a grand hotel that opened in 1922 and has been on the National Register of Historic Places since 1977. It's the only spa available on-site at a hotel within the city limits and thus a favorite among its many bridal parties and wedding guests throughout the year. Boasting an "eclectic array of cross-cultural therapies," the spa treats every guest as a VIP, with warm robes, a mood-setting waiting room, and expertly talented masseuses, estheticians, and makeup and hair artists.

The Spa at the Providence Biltmore
11 Dorrance St., 800-294-7709
providencebiltmore.com/the-spa.html

GET FLORALLY INSPIRED
AT THE RHODE ISLAND FLOWER SHOW

Though it's technically held in February, the Rhode Island Spring Flower & Garden Show will surely get you in the mood for spring and summer with what seems like miles and miles of elaborate flower and garden displays. Each year brings a distinct theme, and exhibitors never cease to amaze with their creative, colorful, and inspiring displays. Past themes have included "Vintage Gardens," which called for creations combining gardens and vintage automobiles, and "Simple Pleasures," which inspired whimsical and timeless garden exhibits. The four-day show also includes lectures, demonstrations, live music, and a preview party. Run by the Rhode Island Horticultural Society, this is an extremely popular event. Consider getting your tickets when they go on sale the October preceding the event.

Rhode Island Spring Flower & Garden Show
Rhode Island Convention Center
One Sabin St., 401-253-0246
flowershow.com

TOUR THE CITY
FROM THE WATER WITH PROVIDENCE RIVER BOAT COMPANY

There's no better way to take in the city's skyline, decorated with architectural greatness as diverse as the city's history and neighborhoods, than from a Providence River Boat Company tour. Onboard the MV *Proud Mary*, a 28' pontoon boat, tour participants get a forty-five-minute tour of the Providence River and harbor, Riverwalk, and Waterplace Park on an afternoon-narrated tour or a sunset tour where cocktails are encouraged (purchased on board). Each pontoon boat seats fourteen to sixteen, but groups can reserve both boats for a party of twenty-eight to thirty people. The company also runs a once-a-year Santa tour, complete with hot cocoa and cookies and a visit from you-know-who, as well as tours during WaterFire lightings.

Providence River Boat Company
575 South Water St., 401-580-BOAT
providenceriverboat.com

TAKE THE FAMILY
TO ROGER WILLIAMS PARK ZOO

One of America's oldest zoos, Roger Williams Park Zoo is a family favorite and will delight visitors of all ages. Within the zoo's forty acres, you'll be able to visit with amphibians, birds, bugs, and mammals, including cheetahs, elephants, giraffes, leopards, red pandas, sloths, and zebras to name only a few. The zoo has seven major exhibit areas. A highlight is the Feinstein Junior Scholar Wetlands Trail, a quarter-mile walking path where native wildlife includes great blue herons and wood ducks, and interactive stations enhance a learning opportunity. Two cafes feature American favorites and some more exotic fare as well as a sweets shop, though it's closed from November to April. Several special events are featured throughout the year, including a Brew at the Zoo beer festival and opportunities to participate in animal feedings.

Roger Williams Park Zoo
1000 Elmwood Ave., 401-941-4998
rwpzoo.org

TIP
Don't miss a ride on the gorgeous Victorian
carousel that has been at the zoo since the 1890s.

CARVE OUT TIME
FOR THE JACK-O-LANTERN SPECTACULAR

One of the several special events offered throughout the year at Roger Williams Park Zoo, the Jack-o-Lantern Spectacular is Halloween-type fun the entire family can enjoy. Each year in October the spectacular work of a few dozen professional and very talented carvers lights the night along the zoo's wetland trails and pond, with pumpkins intricately designed along a theme that in the past has included "All the World's a Stage" and featured *the* kiss from *Gone with the Wind* and "Jack-o-Lanterns A to Z," which featured a carved representation of each letter of the alphabet. The event attracts upwards of 140,000 people from across New England and can get overcrowded, so go early on in the season.

Jack-o-Lantern Spectacular at the Roger Williams Park Zoo
1000 Elmwood Ave., 401-941-4998
rwpzoo.com

BE AWED
AT THE MUSEUM OF NATURAL HISTORY AND PLANETARIUM

Since 1896, Providence's Museum of Natural History and Planetarium has housed a treasure trove of natural history materials and cultural artifacts that represent the evolution of animal species and the environment within the state and a look into the habits, preferences, and belongings of its residents over the last 120 years. The city of Providence operates the museum, which has served as a pseudo state historical museum in the absence of an official one. Its collections include preserved plants and animals, birds and mammals, and a vast archive of historical documents and photographs. The museum's planetarium is open for shows on Saturdays and Sundays only, but additional shows are presented during the city's spring school vacation week and throughout July and August.

1000 Elmwood Ave., 401-680-7221
providenceri.com/museum

BREATHE IN BEAUTY
AT THE ROGER WILLIAMS PARK BOTANICAL CENTER

There's zero chance you won't feel relaxed and more appreciative of all the natural wonder around you after a trip to the Roger Williams Park Botanical Center, which just happens to be at twelve thousand square feet the largest indoor botanical center in New England. Opened by the city of Providence in 2007, the botanical center contains two greenhouses that house more than 150 species of plants and flowers. Almost all were planted by park staff, and you can also enjoy outdoor displays. The center is a delight when perused at your leisure, but you can also take a tour led by master gardener volunteers. Tours educate visitors on the importance of plants and how they adapt to our environment.

Roger Williams Park Botanical Center
1000 Elmwood Ave., 401-785-9450
providenceri.com/botanical-center

BE A KID AGAIN
AT THE PROVIDENCE CHILDREN'S MUSEUM

As the name promises, the focus is on children at this city museum, but watching your little ones delight as they explore the interactive exhibits here surely will make you feel like a kid again yourself. Exhibits and play areas that include chances to discover the magic of water, ice, and mist, to make magnetic mazes, and to travel through Rhode Island's historical timeline are designed to foster all levels of children's development and created to allow children of varying abilities to learn as they play, socialize, construct, and discover. The museum's discovery studio has a rotating schedule of activities where children can create and in some cases take home art and science projects. The museum also hosts several special activity events throughout the year.

Providence Children's Museum
100 South St., 401-273-5437
childrenmuseum.org

TAKE IN AN IVY LEAGUE FOOTBALL GAME
AT BROWN UNIVERSITY

Providence's only Ivy League institution is full of collegiate pride, which is very much on display at the Brown University Brown Bears football games. The Brown Bears play their games at the twenty-thousand-seat Brown Stadium as part of the NCAA Division I Football Championship Subdivision. Plenty of sports history can be taken in at the stadium where National Football League players once played. A real treat would be to score tickets to a Brown home game with the Harvard University Crimson, who play each other in the first game of the Ivy League football season each year. It's noted that whoever wins this game usually does better throughout the season.

Brown Stadium
400 Elmgrove Ave., 401-863-2211
brownbears.com

SPEND A NIGHT
AT THE DEAN HOTEL

Ooh la la. If you're looking for the most Providence-centric of accommodations in town, the boutique Dean Hotel is the place to rest your head. The fifty-two-room hotel prides itself on having re-created a bit of uniquely elegant history downtown, having transformed a long-standing beautiful building into this instantaneous hot spot. Rooms feature a mix of vintage furniture and decor, with some custom artwork and modern amenities. Toilets are made for the hotel only. You won't want to stay in your room all the time, though. The Dean has a beer hall with authentic Bavarian fare, a cocktail den that allows quiet conversation, a karaoke bar, and also a coffee shop. No matter what wets your whistle, you'll be singing the praises of a luxuriously fun hotel.

Dean Hotel
122 Fountain St., 401-455-DEAN
thedeanhotel.com

HAVE A PICNIC OR WALK
AT LIPPITT PARK, PROSPECT TERRACE PARK, OR INDIA POINT PARK

What's better than a picnic lunch on a clear, warm (or cool) day? You're outside, you're taking in the fresh air, and you're surrounded by natural beauty and light. Providence has three parks perfect for the occasion. The city takes great care of its neighborhood parks (not limited to these three), calling them the "heart and soul" of its parks system. While you nibble your lunch atop a blanket, you'll surely see plenty of walkers, runners, bicyclists, and dog walkers enjoying the parks as well. Perhaps you'll join them after lunch?

Lippitt Memorial Park
1059 Hope St.

Prospect Terrace Park
184 Pratt St.

India Point Park
109 India St.
providenceri.com/parks-and-rec/neighborhood-parks

TIP

Don't miss the Roger Williams Memorial at Prospect Terrace Park. Rhode Island's founder, Roger Williams, is buried here in a tomb beneath a statue dedicated to him in the late 1930s.

BE AMAZED
AT WATERFIRE PROVIDENCE

Ah, WaterFire. This has been the can't-miss event in Providence since what began as an art installation to celebrate New Year's Eve turned into a seasonal celebration of what makes Providence a beautiful city at night. Renowned Providence artist Barnaby Evans has created an internationally renowned magical sculptural attraction. About a dozen times during the summer, the Providence River is decorated with nearly one hundred torch-lit vessels that create a scene reminiscent of an old European river city when thousands of visitors and residents stroll Waterplace Park and the Riverwalk to take in this beautiful display. Carefully selected soundtracks only enhance the romanticism often associated with a WaterFire stroll where couples often steal a kiss. Don't worry about impressionable eyes, however. This annual event is completely family friendly, and children of all ages are equally impressed with the display.

WaterFire Providence
101 Regent Ave., 401-273-1155

ROMANCE YOUR SWEETIE
ON A GONDOLA RIDE WITH LA GONDOLA PROVIDENCE

Aboard one of La Gondola Providence's authentic (Italian-made) gondolas, you could almost think you're in Venice, Italy, but why would you want to be in Venice when you have everything you need to be wowed right in front of you? Matthew "Marcello" Haynes founded the company in 2007, which has since gained a national reputation as a wonderful activity for the entire family or for an especially romantic evening. Enjoy a narrated and serenaded ride around the city's riverfront or make an evening reservation, bring a bottle of wine, and prepare for one of Providence's most romantic dates. La Gondola also operates tours during WaterFire lightings, but, as you can imagine, these are very popular, so reserve a spot early, especially if you plan to propose, as this has become quite a popular plan.

La Gondola Providence
One Citizens Plaza, 401-421-8877
lagondolari.com

CELEBRATE AMERICA'S INDEPENDENCE
AT GASPEE DAYS

What says American celebration like a parade? The annual Gaspee Days Parade held on the second Saturday of June in Pawtuxet Village, which straddles the nearby cities of Cranston and Warwick, is surely a testament to all that is American independence, with colonial fife and drum corps, military reenactments, musical groups, and many more revelers. Gaspee Days commemorates the 1772 burning of the HMS *Gaspee*, a British schooner, by Rhode Island patriots in what is described as this country's "first blow for freedom." Rhode Island has been throwing an anniversary party for the event since 1965, when the committee formed to celebrate the two hundredth anniversary of the burning. Gaspee Days is a true family affair, and it's not uncommon to see many generations of Rhode Island families gathered together to join in the events that include an orchestra concert and fireworks, an arts and crafts festival, a 5K road race, and the "burning of the Gaspee" (a remodel, of course).

Gaspee Days Committee
P.O. Box 1772, Warwick, 401-781-1772
gaspee.com

TAKE A DAY TRIP
TO BEAUTIFUL BLOCK ISLAND

The Nature Conservancy has named Block Island one of twelve "Last Great Places" in the Western Hemisphere, and it's so easy to see why, with its beautiful harbor, picturesque New England town roads, and gorgeous beach. Situated in the Atlantic Ocean, fourteen miles south of the Rhode Island coast and thirteen miles east of Montauk Point on Long Island, Block Island is accessible by plane but you want to go by ferry, which you can take from Narragansett or Newport, Rhode Island, or Fall River, Massachusetts, to get the full day across the sea effect. Once you get there, spend some time strolling along the harbor before relaxing on the beach or partaking in awe-inspiring views while bicycling or hiking. Don't miss the island's two historic lighthouses—Block Island North Light and Southeast Light. You might also want to explore all the undeveloped land on the island's northwestern area for a full-on natural experience.

Block Island Ferry
304 Great Island Road, Narragansett, 401-783-7996
blockislandferry.com

GET YOUR SURF ON
AT GOOSEWING BEACH
IN LITTLE COMPTON

You might not immediately associate Rhode Island with surfing, but our Atlantic waters make for some excellent waves. Goosewing Beach in Little Compton, Rhode Island, is a local favorite for amateur surfers because it's usually not crowded and offers the chance to practice without competing for water space. A bonus is that it's really easy to convince non-surfers in your gang to come along, as Goosewing Beach is quiet, off the beaten path, and ideal for a day of total calm and relaxation even in the summer. Another bonus is that the beach makes a great spot for a romantic date, whether it's a daytime picnic or an evening sunset spot.

Goosewing Beach
South Shore Road, Little Compton

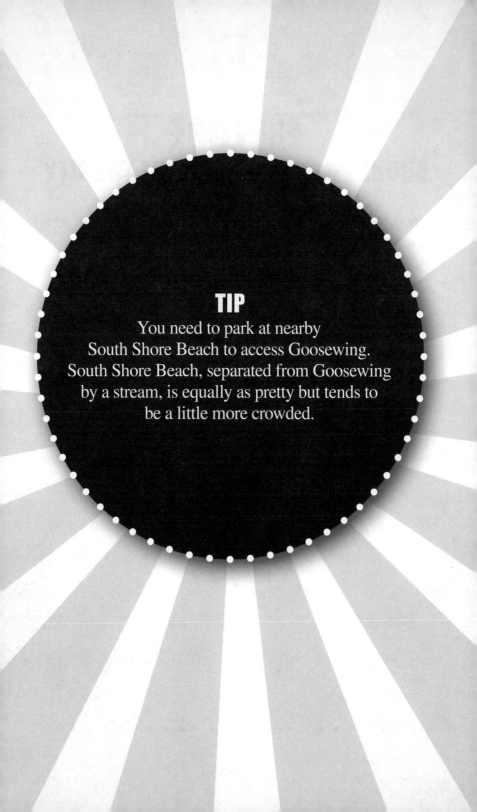

TIP

You need to park at nearby
South Shore Beach to access Goosewing.
South Shore Beach, separated from Goosewing
by a stream, is equally as pretty but tends to
be a little more crowded.

EXPLORE
RHODE ISLAND LIFE OUTSIDE THE CITY

You don't need to leave Providence to experience much of what Rhode Island has to offer, but day trips or weekends to these within-an-hour destinations each offer their own unique attractions, dining, and beauty.

NEWPORT, RI

Gilded-age mansions, unique boutique shops, fine dining, and old-time pubs all share space in historic Newport, Rhode Island. This seaside city was a major shipping port back in the eighteenth century and today is arguably one of the country's top coastal tourist destinations. Also consider touring the Naval War College Museum, the International Tennis Hall of Fame, and the Newport Art Museum.

discovernewport.com

BRISTOL, RI

Rhode Island's smaller mansion-filled tourist destination, Bristol is on par with Newport when it comes to coastal views, exquisite restaurants, and raucous bars. In addition to a lovely Fourth of July parade, Bristol attracts visitors to its waterfront district, the America's Cup Hall of Fame, and Linden Place, a mansion that was once home to two of the country's wealthiest families and was used as a filming location for *The Great Gatsby* starring Robert Redford.

bristolri.com

NARRAGANSETT, RI

Beaches are a big attraction in Narragansett, so you'll likely want to make this day trip during the summer. Three town beaches—Narragansett Town Beach, Scarborough State Beach, and Roger Wheeler State Beach—are pristine and are huge draws for typical day-at-the-beach fun. You'll also want to visit the Point Judith Lighthouse, a working lighthouse since 1810, though it's now automated, and the original structure was destroyed in an 1815 hurricane. (It's since been reconstructed.) Good food is everywhere to be found here, especially when it comes to fresh seafood.

CULTURE AND HISTORY

STUDY GASTRONOMIC HISTORY
AT THE CULINARY ARTS MUSEUM AT JOHNSON & WALES UNIVERSITY

The history of Providence's well-earned foodie reputation is all on display at the Culinary Arts Museum at Johnson & Wales University, a teaching museum with a mission to encourage academic and public study and enjoyment of Rhode Island's hospitality history. From home and industrial kitchen displays to antique restaurant menus and cookbooks, the museum houses over two hundred fifty thousand items, including a reference library of the Retail Bakers of America. A real treat is the museum's permanent display, "Diners: Still Cookin' in the Twenty-First Century," which boasts an actual diner car that visitors can peek into. The museum also hosts lectures and other events throughout the year.

Culinary Arts Museum at Johnson & Wales University
315 Harborside Blvd., Providence, 401-598-2805
culinary.org

BROWSE THROUGH THE CITY
AT GALLERY NIGHT PROVIDENCE

With so many boutique art galleries and museums located throughout the city, gallery goers and art fans have long turned to Gallery Night, a monthly guided tour of art spaces around town to discover new gems and friends. On the third Thursday of the month (from March through November), patrons gather and are transported by bus to neighborhood galleries and other art spaces. Participating galleries most often greet visitors with wine and cheese to enjoy while browsing the works of talented local artists. Guests can take guided tours at each stop or explore each space on their own. Some nights also include historical site visits, and all buses are staffed with guides, many of whom are local artists.

One Regency Plaza Providence, 401-490-2042
gallerynight.org

JOHN BROWN
HOUSE MUSEUM

One of two museums maintained by the Rhode Island Historical Society, the John Brown House is the first mansion built in Providence and offers a beautiful account of what Providence looked like in the late eighteenth century. John Brown, an early American merchant and cofounder of Brown University, built his mansion in 1786 and is rumored to have hosted President George Washington for tea in the home. Renovated under a new owner to include modern bathrooms and heating, the Brown family regained ownership of the mansion in 1936 and donated it to the historical society in 1942. The society has preserved the building and restored its original colonial decor. The building maintains eleven original mantelpieces and many original furnishings. The building was declared a national historical landmark in 1968.

John Brown House Museum
52 Power St., Providence, 401-273-7507
rihs.org

CHECK OUT
THE PROVIDENCE PUBLIC LIBRARY

Turn-of-the-century architecture with a gorgeous interior welcomes patrons to the Providence Public Library, a 140-year-old (built in 1900) operating library downtown. The library's grand and storied halls and rooms holds print, recorded, and digital collections available to any cardholding resident. Under new directorship in recent years, the library has also become a center for creative events and community programming that centers on offering low-cost and free learning opportunities, including lectures, discussions, and workshops. Regularly changing exhibits are often centered on specific aspects of the state's history. History buffs might be interested in guided tours of the library, offered at 10:30 a.m. on the first and third Tuesday of each month.

150 Empire St., Providence, 401-455-8000
provlib.org

JOIN THE FESTIVAL
OF HISTORIC HOUSES

The Providence Preservation Society's annual Festival of Historic Houses is a can't-miss event for lovers of history, architecture, and beauty. Traditionally held over a weekend each June, the tour allows access to otherwise off-limits historical houses in the city, though the tour theme changes from year to year. A recent tour highlighted Fox Point neighborhood homes that showcased modern living in historical spaces and featured more than a dozen residences and gardens. As if this tour weren't enough, the weekend also includes a Friday night party at a Providence historical site that doubles as a fund-raiser for the preservation society.

Providence Preservation Society
21 Meeting St., #2, Providence, 401-831-7440
ppsri.org

TAKE A WALK
ON THE EAST SIDE

When Roger Williams founded Providence in 1636, he did so along College Hill, one of the neighborhoods comprising the city's East Side, thus making a walking tour through this city section a historical and beautiful one. Thanks to GoProvidence, the city's convention and visitor's bureau, residents and visitors can guide themselves through such spots as the Roger Williams National Memorial, the Old Brick School House, the Providence Art Club, the Market House, and the Stephen Hopkins House, to name just a few. The walk will also take you down several historical streets, such as George Street, which is lined with Victorian and Georgian homes. Use the downloadable map at goprovidence.com to select all or some of the sites for your tour. GoProvidence also has lots of suggestions for a food and drink break along the way.

GoProvidence
10 Memorial Boulevard, Providence, 401-456-0200
goprovidence.com

VISIT
THE RISD MUSEUM

The Rhode Island School of Design, one of the country's premier art and design higher educational institutions, primes talented, creative, and ambitious artists for their careers. The school also hosts a museum dedicated to showcasing, among other exhibits, the works of this nation's up-and-coming star artists. With seven permanent collections spanning five buildings, the museum is home to around one hundred thousand objects, including ancient art, Asian art, contemporary art, costume and textiles, decorative arts and design, painting and sculpture, and prints, drawings, and photographs. Easily the most recognizable art museum in Rhode Island, its temporary exhibits regularly draw crowds as do special events, such as open studio and art and design nights, among other monthly offerings.

RISD Museum
224 Benefit St., Providence, 401-454-6500
risdmuseum.org

TIP

The RISD Museum stays open later on the
third Thursday of every month, until 9 p.m.,
when crowds are usually smaller. Don't forget
to visit the museum's gift shop, RISD Works,
to browse and purchase student work.

NORTH BURIAL GROUND TOUR

Providence's largest municipal cemetery, the North Burial Ground, has been the final resting place of some of the city's most prominent historical figures since 1700. As happened across much of the region, the cemetery was landscaped in the nineteenth century to be of use for recreational activities and it remains a popular spot for walking and jogging among its windy hills and varied gravesite sculptures. Maps of notable graves and memorials are available to visitors, who can visit the burial ground, which occupies 109 acres on the city's East Side, seven days a week from 8:30 a.m. to 4:30 p.m. Virtual maps are available through Rhode Island College, where a recent multidisciplinary project has focused on promoting the cemetery as a valuable economic and educational asset. More than thirty-five thousand are buried here, including many Rhode Island governors and other political figures.

NOTABLE BURIALS

Zachariah Allen, Providence mill owner and civic leader

John Brown, merchant and cofounder of Brown University

Kady Brownell, Civil War veteran

Charles Dow, journalist, cofounder of Dow Jones & Company, and founder of the *Wall Street Journal*

Albert Martin, only Rhode Islander to fight at the Battle of the Alamo

Annie Smith Peck, pioneer and mountaineer

Sam Walter Foss, poet

Sarah Helen Whitman, poet, essayist, and romantic partner of Edgar Allan Poe

NORTH BURIAL GROUND

5 Branch Ave., Providence, 401-331-0177
ric.edu/northburialground

TOUR THE RHODE ISLAND STATE HOUSE

Rhode Island may be a small state, but among its boasts is having the third-largest self-supporting dome in the world (behind only St. Peter's Basilica and the Taj Mahal), which tops the rotunda at the state house. Made of white Georgia marble and brick, the state house sits on a hill overlooking downtown and is a stunning piece of neoclassical architecture. The interior is equally impressive, and visitors can take a guided tour of the state house, including the rotunda, several times per day, Monday through Friday except holidays. Stops on the tour include the State Room, where Gilbert Stuart's portrait of George Washington hangs, and the Bell Room, where a replica of the Liberty Bell is displayed.

Rhode Island State House
82 Smith St., Providence, 401-222-3983
sos.ri.gov/publicinfo/tours/

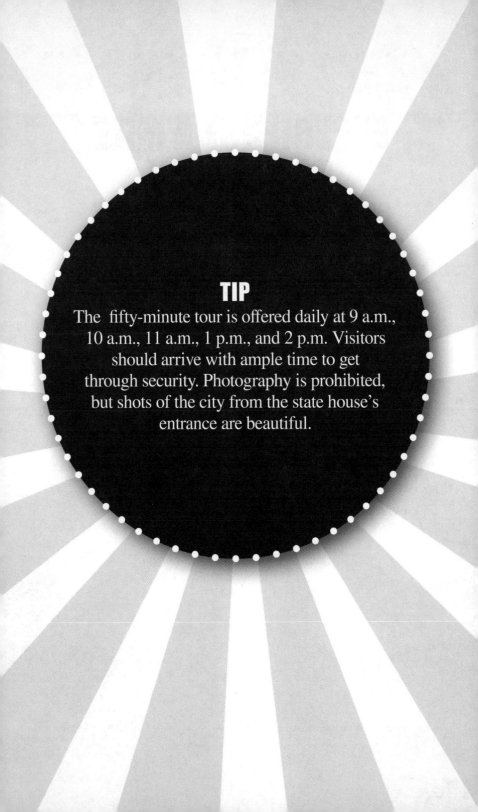

TIP

The fifty-minute tour is offered daily at 9 a.m., 10 a.m., 11 a.m., 1 p.m., and 2 p.m. Visitors should arrive with ample time to get through security. Photography is prohibited, but shots of the city from the state house's entrance are beautiful.

EXPERIENCE A MILE OF HISTORY
ON THE BENEFIT STREET TOUR

The warmer season brings the Rhode Island Historical Society's annual guided street tours, usually offered from June through October. Among these is the "Benefit Street: A Mile of History" walking tour, which offers participants a view into this historic street that was, according to the historical society, created "for the benefit of all." Colonial homes line a cobblestone street that has been the focus of preservation efforts since the 1950s. While visitors often feel like they are walking through history, Benefit Street is filled with residences, shops, and restaurants that have kept the neighborhood imperative to Providence's economic development. The historical society also offers themed tours during the season that are centered on Providence's literary and women's history.

Rhode Island Historical Society
Begins at John Brown House Museum
52 Power St., Providence
rihs.org

EXPLORE
THE STEEL YARD

Whether you're interested in making art or celebrating it—or both—the Steel Yard in nearby Seekonk, Massachusetts, is sure to get your creative energy flowing with a plethora of available workspaces, classes, and events centered on its mission to be an "environment of experimentation." Founded as a nonprofit in 2001 at the former Providence Steel and Iron complex, the Steel Yard was envisioned as a place for the incubation and education of how innovation can be used to revitalize the urban economy through art and community. Today, artists and entrepreneurs from all walks of life use the space to create and build a collaborative network to move their work forward. The Steel Yard holds classes in blacksmithing, welding, jewelry making, and ceramics as well as exceptional local artist exhibits.

The Steel Yard
27 Sims Ave., Seekonk, 401-273-7101
thesteelyard.org

CHECK INTO
THE PROVIDENCE ATHENAEUM

Visitors to the Providence Athenaeum marvel at the library's wondrous stacks that invoke the feeling of being inside an eighteenth-century European treasure trove of literature. The library was founded in 1836 as "the Athenaeum" from the Providence Library Company and the Providence Athenaeum and remains an operating, member-supported library and cultural center that prides itself on welcoming all who love reading and history to connect at the cultural center. The public is welcome to browse the Athenaeum's collections and encourages membership for those who wish to check out materials. The library also holds programs meant to bring together the public to engage in learning and to preserve its historic building, which is encompassed in a marvelous stone exterior.

Providence Athenaeum
251 Benefit St., Providence, 401-421-6970
providenceathenaeum.org

SEE TOMORROW'S STARS OF STAGE AND SCREEN
AT RHODE ISLAND COLLEGE

The performing and fine arts department at Rhode Island College, the state's oldest public higher education institution, annually showcases student and faculty talent through its Performing Arts Series and music, theater and dance events. With three well-constructed performing venues on campus, each season presents a bounty of opportunities to take in dance, music, and theatrical productions at a low cost. It also presents the chance to see tomorrow's stars as they get their start. Tony award–winning actress Viola Davis famously got her start on stage at Rhode Island College.

Rhode Island College
600 Mt. Pleasant Ave., Providence, 401-456-8144
ric.edu/pfa

GET INTO LITERARY HISTORY
ON THE H. P. LOVECRAFT TOUR

Providence's claim to literary fame rests heavily on the late Howard Phillips (H. P.) Lovecraft, who lived in poverty but lives on through a cult following and as a renowned author of horror fiction. He lived and died (at age forty-six in 1937) in Providence and is buried in the Swan Point Cemetery on Blackstone Boulevard. Lovecraft's gravesite is only one of many spots that have significance to the author's legacy. In the past, the annual FLICKERS: Vortex Sci-Fi, Fantasy & Horror Film Festival (with help from the Rhode Island Historical Society) has held a guided walking tour to the cemetery, the site of his former home, and landmarks he wrote about in his books, including Prospect Terrace and the First Baptist Church. The festival traditionally happens each October, but maps are available if you want to take this eerily thrilling tour yourself at any other time of year.

H. P. Lovecraft Tour
FLICKERS: Vortex Sci-Fi, Fantasy & Horror Film Festival
83 Park St., Suite 5, Providence, 401-490-6735
film-festival.org/HPLovecraft14.php

FIRST BAPTIST CHURCH

Providence's First Baptist Church, also known as the First Baptist Meeting House, is the oldest Baptist church congregation in America and is a must-see sight for any visitor or resident. Founded by Roger Williams in 1638, just two years after he founded Providence, the building as it stands on North Main Street was built in 1774 and was used as a meeting house beginning in May 1775. Unlike Baptist buildings of the time, the church was erected with a steeple and bell that reflected an eighteenth-century urban movement for acceptance of Baptists. Weekly services are still held at the meetinghouse on Sundays, and guided tours are available by reservation from Memorial Day through Columbus Day. Visitors can also take self-guided tours of the church throughout the rest of the year as well as following Sunday services.

First Baptist Church
75 N Main St., Providence, 401-454-3418
firstbaptistchurchinamerica.org

BE DAZZLED
AT THE PROVIDENCE
INTERNATIONAL ARTS FESTIVAL

The Providence International Arts Festival is a collaboration between the city of Providence and FirstWorks, a local arts organization, meant to showcase local and international artists as well as ties between them. The festival's main attraction is on Saturday when a full day of events unites almost the entire downtown with stages set up throughout. Block parties abound, and evening activities follow. The fun starts earlier in the week, however, with events across the city, including conversations and panels, dance parties, musical performances, and gallery exhibitions. The festival also includes an opening night party (which previously has been held at the Providence Biltmore) that ties in with events at performance spaces and theaters.

Providence International Arts Festival
Various locations, 401-421-4278
first-works.org

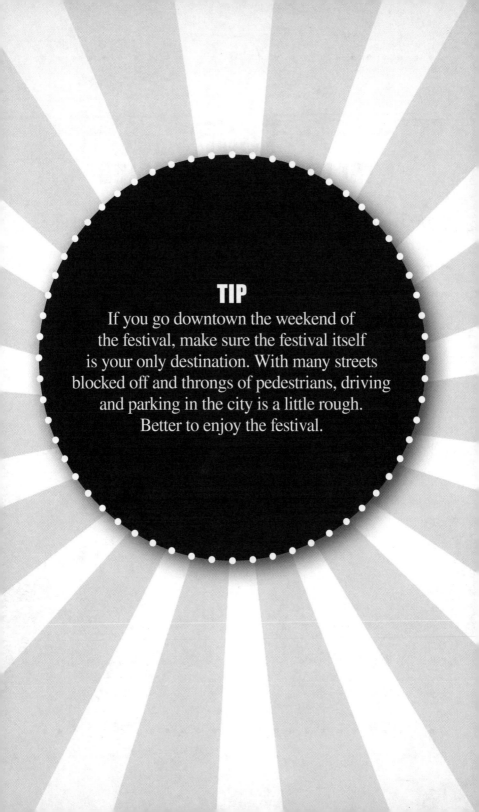

TIP

If you go downtown the weekend of
the festival, make sure the festival itself
is your only destination. With many streets
blocked off and throngs of pedestrians, driving
and parking in the city is a little rough.
Better to enjoy the festival.

TOUR
THE PROVIDENCE ART CLUB

The Providence Art Club, founded in 1880, is both an exclusive membership club and a gallery space that offers free exhibitions to the general public. Exhibitions—and there are many throughout the year—are centered on fostering appreciation for art and artists. The building, the club's home since 1887, is one of many historic houses that line Thomas Street and the club's Reading Room is paneled with the home's original wooden shutters. Though it's not verified, the Providence Art Club is thought to the oldest such club in the nation. It was founded by sixteen men and women who wanted to establish what today is known as an artist's cooperative, where they could gather, work, and exhibit their work.

Providence Art Club
11 Thomas St., 401-331-1114
providenceartclub.org

VISIT
THE HOME OF A DECLARATION SIGNER AT THE STEPHEN HOPKINS HOUSE

Stephen Hopkins, a Rhode Island native, was one of two delegates to the First Continental Congress and in 1776 singed the Declaration of Independence for Rhode Island. Guided tours of his family home are offered from May through November. The home features a bedchamber where George Washington once slept. Hopkins had a political career, starting at age twenty-four when he was elected town solicitor in Scituate, Rhode Island. He served in the General Assembly for Scituate before moving to Providence and serving as a delegate to the Congress of Albany, where he teamed with Benjamin Franklin to advocate for the union. He also published "The Rights of Colonies Examined," which denounced the Stamp Act.

Stephen Hopkins House
15 Hopkins St., 401-421-0694
stephenhopkins.org

RELIVE RHODY HISTORY
AT THE ROCKY POINT CLAM SHACK

Rhode Islanders are still mourning the demise of Rocky Point, a once lively amusement park that closed in 1996 but has forever found a place in the hearts of everyone in little Rhody. Who can blame them? The theme park with its traditional roller coasters, penny arcade, Ferris wheel, and famed dinner hall was the place for family fun for more than 150 years. In re-creating some of that magic at the Rocky Point Clam Shack in nearby Warwick, owner Anthony Restivo has given Rhode Islanders a new place to create memories and share good old-fashioned Ocean State treats. It doesn't hurt that the shack is decorated with memorabilia from of the park, but the menu created with some of the Old Shore Dinner Hall favorites in mind is what really has everyone's mouths watering.

Rocky Point Clam Shack
1689 Post Rd., Warwick, 401-738-9830
rockypointclamshack.com

TIP

The outdoor restaurant is only open from spring through early fall, but when in season be sure to get the true Rocky Point experience and order the red chowder and clam cakes.

SHOPPING AND FASHION

PASS THE BREAD
AT SEVEN STARS BAKERY

Providence's go-to East Side bakery opened in January 2001 with the mission to "bake great stuff and treat our customers well." Mission accomplished. Locals flock to Seven Stars Bakery all day to treat themselves to pastries, cookies, and muffins and to pick up any of the bakery's seven bread varieties, including the very popular durum loaf and stick, a rustic bread with a crunchy but chewy crust. The shop also serves coffee, and locals love to sit and talk over a croissant or Danish. The shop is incredibly popular during holidays, so if you want to bring a delectable bread to your party, take advantage of the shop's option to order ahead.

Seven Stars Bakery—two locations
820 Hope St., 342 Broadway, 401-521-2200
sevenstarsbakery.com

BROWSE THE STACKS
AT SYMPOSIUM BOOKS

This independent bookstore caters to the intellectual and artistic shoppers seeking those can't-find-in-a-big-name-store titles. The Symposium's decor and vibe enhance its reputation as a shop for the non-shoppers, where an eclectic mix of music encourages long periods of browsing, skimming, and chatting with staff who are always happy to help shoppers select something for themselves or a gift for the hard-to-please person on their list. Booklovers adore seeing the wide range of books on the store shelves, from architecture and business to philosophy, poetry, and fiction. Plenty of knickknacks to suit many tastes are available as well, but if you're after more of the kid-friendly inventory, visit the shop's second location in East Greenwich.

Symposium Books
240 Westminster St., Providence, 401-273-7900
symposiumbooks.com

VISIT AMERICA'S FIRST INDOOR MALL
AT THE ARCADE

Once America's oldest operating indoor shopping mall, the Arcade was built in 1828 and, after several reincarnations for various purposes, had been vacant for several years until it recently reopened as a combination shopping/dining and residential building. Through it all, the building has been one of downtown's most admired architectural centerpieces. Now, a few dozen micro-loft apartments occupy the Arcade's upper floors, while shops such as Nude, a haven for local designers and their fans, and eateries such as the heavily locally sourced Rogue Island Kitchen share space on the first floor. Locals and visitors love feeling the pulse of the city's history as they browse through the shops and as they dine here.

The Arcade Providence
65 Weybosett St., 401-454-4568
arcadeprovidence.com

SHOP ECO-FRIENDLY
AT RESTORED BY DESIGN

If there were a section of heaven specifically designed for fashionistas and shopaholics who want their clothing, accessories, and homewares to reflect their eco-friendly lifestyle, Restored by Design would surely be its flagship shop. A self-described "green artisan company," Restored by Design is much more than a unique boutique. The shop focuses on selling locally made pieces that are made from existing objects—think repurposed vintage finds. Restored by Design also offers classes in sewing and jewelry making and in making your own repurposed pieces, as well as orders for custom design. Visitors wanting to take home a piece of Providence won't be disappointed here—no imports allowed.

Restored by Design
128 N Main St., 401-241-2143
restoredbydesign.com

GET YOUR BEAUTY FIX
AT SERRECCHIA BOUTIQUE

An ideal stop for bath-and-skin care fanatics and those shopping for them, Serrecchia Boutique features a plethora of products for both men and women, including skin care, cosmetics, and shave creams. The shop is focused on carrying unique products and follows through on that mission with an eclectic array of beauty products, perfume, accessories, and clothing with an emphasis on dance wear. Though not every product is locally made, Serrecchia Boutique does carry many Rhode Island–made items, including soaps from Shore Soap Co., a husband-and-wife shop out of Newport. Plus, if you're lucky, you might happen in during one of the shop's promotional events that are known to feature belly dancers.

Serrecchia Boutique
464 Wickenden St., 401-519-4506
serrechiaboutique.com

INVEST IN TOMORROW'S FAMOUS ARTISTS
AT RISD WORKS

Want to own a piece of art before the artist becomes famous? Or invest in the continuation of art and design education? RISD Works, the museum shop at the Rhode Island School of Design, exclusively carries items designed and made by RISD alumni and faculty. This includes merchandise coordinated with museum exhibitions and collections. Items run the full spectrum of RISD-offered degrees, and that's nineteen art-centered disciplines, so there's sure to be something for everyone, from fine art and prints to home accessories, jewelry, books, and children's gifts. Some RISD Works items are available for purchase online, but you'd really be missing out if you don't stop in and browse the take-home masterpieces.

RISD Works
20 North Main St., 401-277-4949
risdworks.com

PICK UP
SOMETHING ARTFUL
AT GALLERY Z

If a visit to Providence allows you time to see only one independent gallery, Gallery Z needs to be the one. If you're a Providence area resident and haven't been there yet, the time is now. Located on Federal Hill, the gallery has an amazingly large and varied collection of original fine art, including paintings, photographs, drawings, and sculptures as well as jewelry and pottery. The gallery includes works from national and international artists but also local artists and hosts several exhibitions throughout the year. Just be sure to plan your visit. The gallery is open only Thursdays through Saturdays from noon to 8 p.m. and every third and last Sunday of the month from noon to 6 p.m. From Mondays to Wednesdays, you can make an appointment or hope someone's working when you stop by.

Gallery Z
259 Atwells Ave., 401-454-8844
galleryzprov.com

GET FRESH VEGGIES
AND MUCH MORE AT HOPE STREET FARMERS MARKET

May through October is a very happy time indeed for fans—and there are many of them—of the Hope Street Farmers Market, a farmer-fun cooperative that takes over Lippitt Park Saturdays from 9 a.m. to 1 p.m. and Wednesdays from 3 p.m. to 6 p.m. There are way too many wonderful vendors to mention, but the more important message is that you could grocery shop for a week's worth of veggies, cheeses, breads, sauces, meats, and fish at the market. You can also browse local artisan booths, grab a locally brewed coffee, sample local restaurant fare, and listen to some great local artists serenade the crowd. There's also a bicycle valet and a knife-sharpening station. Really, it doesn't get any better than this.

Hope Street Farmers Market
Lippitt Park, 1015 Hope St., Providence
hopestreetmarket.com

TASTE TONIGHT'S WINE BEFORE YOU BUY
AT BIN 312, CORK & BREW & SPIRITS TOO, BOTTLES FINE WINE, NIKKI'S LIQUORS, AND GASBARRO'S WINES

Toward the end of the workweek and on Saturdays, several local and popular boutique wine and craft beer shops turn into tasting rooms by offering customers the chance to taste affordable and recommended varietals before purchase. Bin 312 sticks to Thursday evening tastings, and Cork & Brew holds Friday evening tastings, while Bottles Fine Wine and Nikki's Liquors are true to late Saturday afternoons. Gasbarro's Wine doesn't host a tasting each week; however, when they do have a tasting, patrons get to taste up to six wines (instead of four wines at most others) thanks to a grandfather clause in the liquor laws. Use your sipping time to browse these shops, where owners and staff are superknowledgeable and ready to recommend something in the unlikely event you don't find a favorite among the samples.

Bin 312
312 South Main St., 401-714-0040
bin312.com

Bottles Fine Wine
141 Pitman St., 401-372-2030
bottlesfinewine.com

Cork & Brew & Spirits Too
2200 Broad St., Cranston, 401-781-1919
corkandbrewandspiritstoo.com

Gasbarro's Wines
361 Atwells Ave., 401-421-4170
gasbarros.com

Nikki's Liquors
32 Branch Ave., 401-861-9006
nikkisliquors.com

TAKE SOME OF FEDERAL HILL HOME
AT VENDA RAVIOLI

Noshing on authentic Italian cuisine and desserts at Costantino's Venda Bar & Ristorante on Federal Hill often has patrons wishing they could cook like its chefs at home. Since that might be a stretch, Costantino's lovers are lucky indeed that Venda Ravioli, the restaurant's emporium, lets customers take home gourmet pastas (that naturally include Venda raviolis), sauces, meats, cheeses, oils and vinegars, and much more. Even those who haven't been to Costantino's (and you should go now) are sure to love browsing this Italian grocery store that also sells Rhode Island–made items, cookbooks, and grocery items. The shop also has specialty Italian gift baskets if you're looking for a great hostess or housewarming gift.

Venda Ravioli
275 Atwells Ave., 401-421-9105
vendaravioli.com

A FOODIE'S DELIGHT
AT STOCK CULINARY GOODS

When Stock Culinary Goods opened on Hope Street a few years ago and said "come on in," foodies across Rhode Island let out a collective roar of adulation, and it's possible some mouths are still open in awe of this delight of a store. With a mission to stock "thoughtfully sourced" and well-made kitchen and gift items, Stock Culinary Goods is a mini-mecca for chefs and those who love them and can rival any big-name kitchenware carrier. Plenty of Rhode Island–made items are to be found among the artfully displayed collection of kitchen tools, drinkware, serving dishes, unique and healthful food items, candles, kitchen linens, and so much more.

Stock Culinary Goods
756 Hope St., 401-521-0101
stockculinarygoods.com

GET UNIQUE GIFTS
AT FROG AND TOAD

If you're looking to take home a kitschy or cute Rhode Island–themed mug, poster, or T-shirt that the locals have in their homes and closets, Frog and Toad on Hope Street is a must-stop on your Providence shopping trip. Founded about ten years ago as a neighborhood shop, Frog and Toad has become quite the popular go-to store for souvenirs, presents, and retail therapy. It has consistently been voted best gift store in the state by *Rhode Island Monthly* readers, and it's easy to see why immediately upon entering. It's almost never the same store twice, with a rotating inventory of knickknacks, jewelry, handmade clothing, handbags, and table linens plus a pretty good selection of children's toys and books. And, of course, there's all the Rhode Island–made souvenirs.

Frog and Toad
795 Hope St., 401-831-3434
frogandtoadstore.com

SHOP FOR THE KIDS
AT CREATOVITY

Why didn't they make toys like these when I was a kid? That's likely to be the exact thing you'll think while shopping at Creatovity, a Hope Street children's toy store that focuses its stock on high-quality games and crafts that include educational stimulants and promote creativity. Some three thousand products are available here for all ages—from infants to teens and beyond—from around the world. You'll recognize some brands, such as Alex and Klutz, but are sure to discover even more. The store also has a noteworthy selection of infant clothing and books and a friendly staff who are great resources when shopping for that hard-to-please child or teen. Complimentary gift wrapping on any in-store purchase is a nice touch too.

Creatovity
736 Hope St., 401-351-5718
creatovity.com

GET CRAFTY
AT CRAFTLAND

What started more than a decade ago as a holiday sale has become a staple of the downtown Providence shopping scene on Westminster Street, offering a place to "celebrate all kinds of sparkly handmade objects and the people who make them." It is, true to its word, a land of crafts with inventory that sparkles either in looks or originality—most times both. Looking for the perfect, locally made greeting card you won't find in a chain store's aisles? It's here. Looking for a journal decorated with a Providence map you won't find anywhere else? It's here. With a heavy selection of Rhode Island–made and –themed gifts and apparel, the shop is a tribute to area crafts people. You can also find baubles, home goods, prints, and clothing, including adorable onesies, so even the littlest Little Rhodys can sport their pride.

Craftland
212 Westminster St., 401-272-4285
craftlandshop.com

HOMESTYLE

Does your home have style? If not, it might be because you haven't been to Homestyle on Westminster Street, the realization of interior decorator Lisa Newman Paratore's expert vision of offering affordably priced unique furniture, home goods, and gifts. When the shop opened in spring 2007, it garnered a slew of Best New and Best Home Accessories awards from *Boston Globe Magazine*, *Rhode Island Monthly*, and *New England Travel*. The accolades only accent the shop's design-inspired atmosphere where customers can get expert advice or simply browse the diverse arrangement of items. You'll find kids monster slippers near peacock-designed wrapping paper and Jonathan Adler decorative bowls. If you like Lisa's store style, hop on over to lisanewmaninteriors.com for a look at her design business.

Homestyle
229 Westminster St., 401-277-1159
homestyleri.com

GET DAPPER DUDS
AT MARC ALLEN

Marc Allen is a must-visit shop for the dapper dude looking for his next dandy-inspired shirt, jacket, pants, tie, or scarf. Marc Streisand, president of Marc Allen Fine Clothiers, has set up a shop that expertly reflects his belief that a man's wardrobe should be a work of art. As such, he and master clothier David Morra help Providence's finest-clad gentlemen find their signature look through a ready-to-wear line and custom suits, sport coats, formal wear, trousers, and shirts. You're in very fine dressing hands here. Streisand brings more than twenty-five years of experience to the company, while Morra, also an experienced tradesman, has dressed very high-profile clients, from professional athletes to local celebrities.

Marc Allen
200 South Main St., 401-453-0025
marcalleninc.com

SAY CHEESE, PLEASE,
FOR NARRAGANSETT CREAMERY

It's trite to say that a company can offer something for everyone, but at Narragansett Creamery it's true and then some. A variety of options are available at many area supermarkets and patrons are bound to find more than one they love . There's the buttery-smelling mozzarella, the steam kettle–heated renaissance ricotta, the crisp queso blanco, the gouda-style divine Providence, and the Italian-style Atwells gold, to name only a few. Rhode Island's Federico family had operated Providence Specialty Products for years before launching the cheese line in 2007, but it didn't take nearly as long for the cheeses to gain an almost cult-like following. If you take one Providence perishable home with you, it's got to be this cheese.

Narragansett Creamery
Various Locations, 401-272-4944
richeeses.com

DECORATE YOUR WALLS
AT PROVIDENCE PICTURE FRAME

Whether you have a special photograph, print, or original art piece to frame or you're looking for something artful to add to your walls, Providence Picture Frame has want you want and then some. It's a big store—a gallery and workshop occupy an acre of space inside the Dryden Lane spot where the focus is providing top-notch customer service with an emphasis on helping patrons discover their personal art style with which to fill their home. Independent artists love utilizing the storefront and its website to display and sell their creations. Customers love being able to both browse with ease and create their own works of art through online tools and then have them custom printed and expertly framed.

Providence Picture Frame
27 Dryden Lane, 401-421-6196
providencepictureframe.com

BOOKS ON THE SQUARE

From bestsellers to regional debuts, Books on the Square in Wayland Square, a popular urban neighborhood, has been a local booklover's paradise since 1992. A serious community ambiance is present inside the small shop, which also stocks plenty of puzzles, cookbooks, children's books, and gifts. This is enhanced by the regular schedule of events, including author visits and signings, an annual Halloween party, weekly story times, and book clubs. If you can't make it in, the shop takes phone orders even for single-copy special orders. The laid-back atmosphere is made for browsing and though the staff always have excellent recommendations, there's no push to buy, but you likely won't need any encouragement.

Books on the Square
471 Angell St., 401-331-9097
booksq.com

SUGGESTED
ITINERARIES

DATE NIGHT

Star Chef's Series at Gracie's, 18

Take in a Broadway Show at the Providence Performing Arts Center, 34

Experience Intimate Theater at Trinity Repertory Company and the Gamm, 35

Take in a Movie at Cable Car Cinema, 38

Have a Jazzy Night at Aspire, 51

Spend a Night at the Dean Hotel, 67

Have a Picnic or Walk at Lippitt Park, Prospect Terrace Park, or India Point Park, 68

Be Amazed at WaterFire Providence, 70

Romance Your Sweetie on a Gondola Ride with La Gondola Providence, 71

OUTDOOR FUN

Ice-Skate under the Stars at the Alex and Ani City Center, 57

Feel Young Again at Wickenden Pub, 22

Vino, Please, 28

GIRLS DAY/NIGHT OUT

Have a Bubbly Brunch at the Duck & Bunny, 8

Visit Southern Italy at Zooma Trattoria, 26

Take in a Broadway Show at the Providence Performing
Arts Center, 34

Pamper Yourself at the Spa at the Providence Biltmore, 58

Get Your Beauty Fix at Serrecchia Boutique, 110

MUSIC LOVERS

Ballet, Music, and More at Veterans Memorial Auditorium, 39

Discover Local Bands at the Met, The Parlour, the SPOT
Underground, and Fête Music Hall, 42

Get Cultured at the Rhode Island Philharmonic Orchestra, 48

Rock out at the Columbus Theatre, 50

Have a Jazzy Night at Aspire, 51

FOODIE FANATICS

HISTORY BUFFS

ACTIVITIES
BY SEASON

WINTER

Discover the Beers the Locals Crave at the Rhode Island Brew Fest, 6

Try a Different Dish Every Night at the Restaurant Week, 23

Get Your Fashionista Fix at Styleweek Northeast, 36

Cheer on the Providence Bruins at the Dunkin' Donuts Center, 56

Ice-Skate under the Stars at the Alex and Ani City Center, 57

SPRING

Indulge in a Culinary Tour of Federal Hill, 2

Grab a Food Truck Lunch at Kennedy Plaza, 5

Cheer on the Girls at the Providence Roller Derby, 45

Get Florally Inspired at the Rhode Island Flower Show, 59

SUMMER

Indulge in a Culinary Tour of Federal Hill, 2

Feast on Fish at the Rhode Island Seafood Festival, 4

FALL

INDEX